PEARLS
OF
WISDOM
FOR THE YOUNG

Kingsley Eleweke

COPYRIGHT

Contact the Author

Email: Primedgesolutions@gmail.com

DEDICATION

This book is dedicated to all the young people out there

who are striving for a fuller and more fulfilling life.

TABLE OF CONTENTS

COPYRIGHT   ii

DEDICATION   iii

TABLE OF CONTENTS   v

PREFACE   vii

DON'T GIVE UP   9

TAKE CHARGE NOW   12

CHALLENGES ARE TEACHERS   16

CHALLENGES ARE ESSENTIAL TO SUCCESS   20

BELIEVE IN YOURSELF   24

TRY AGAIN   26

FOCUS ON THE VICTORY AHEAD   29

IGNORANCE JUSTIFIES NO ONE   32

CONCLUSION   35

ABOUT THE AUTHOR   38

PREFACE

Extraordinary effort breaks barriers to give an unusual result. This world will not give you what you deserve. But by extraordinary determination, you can break boundaries to get an astonishing victory.

My primary aim in writing this book is to inspire every young person to aspire to a fuller and more fulfilling life. I want you to know that you are stronger than what life throws at you. And you possess skills that can proffer solutions to the problems in the world today.

Whatever life has handed you, the only way forward is to resist the temptation of giving up. Your hazy today should not blur your vision of a brighter tomorrow. And rather than looking for a short-term solution, fight. No one desiring a permanent victory seeks a temporary escape; fight with tenacity until you attain your long-term victory.

There is no victory in succumbing to failure and allowing your glorious tomorrow to be clouded with today's defeat. Your setback today is a stepping stone to a prosperous tomorrow. Don't allow disappointments to blur your vision of victory.

If you choose to think differently today, you will distinguish yourself from most today's youth who have surrendered to intoxicating forgetfulness. Consider obstacles as guides sent to lead you to a pearl of higher wisdom and as tools to build the castle of your destiny.

I hope that at the end of this book, you would have found the courage and faith in yourself to work on the aspects of your life that you don't like. Place your today, tomorrow, and all the tomorrows of your life with perfect confidence in the care of God.

CHAPTER ONE
DON'T GIVE UP

Dear friend, I am aware you have challenges you are currently going through. Unfavourable social structures and environmental conditions are impeding your efforts. Though you have made noble efforts, nothing is improving; every time you take a step forward, it seems that you are pulled two steps backwards by an unseen force. However, as long as you are a human, challenges are bound to come your way. You met challenges when you were a baby, but you overcame to develop into a fully grown adult. Since everyone must deal with life's demands to live a richer life, no one is exempt from them.

A famous saying goes by, "Winners do not quit, and quitters do not win." And that is true! If you are a quitter, you will not prevail in the battles of life. Whether you are ready for them or not, trials will inevitably come your way.

Though you are currently going through life a trial, your life is not yet over. Some other people, like you, have experienced the same trials facing you now. Like you, these men and women had challenges, but they overcame those incapacitating and life-threatening obstacles to accomplish some of history's greatest achievements.

Why should you stop trying? Whatever challenges life hands you, you can overcome. You are a fighter, and fighters don't fear conflict. Fight for your freedom and see your difficulty as an opportunity to advance to a higher level. Do not permit your battleground to become your burial ground. It is on the battlefields that champions are created. They emerge from battles with a triumphant shout. When faced with challenges and opponents, champions do not give up easily, as most of us do.

Reaching your goals and overcoming obstacles are both possible. You can overcome poverty and find lasting peace and happiness; hang in there and keep fighting with confidence in yourself until you succeed. Though, circumstances and environmental factors might not always be right. But you have the power to use them as stepping stones to the ideal condition or environment that you desire.

Take your destiny in your hand. Fight the battles of your life bravery with a faith that accepts no defeat. Take responsibility and take charge of your life. There is hope. Don't give up on yourself!

CHAPTER TWO
TAKE CHARGE NOW

Within you is a great power that can make dreams come true. That power can elevate you to a new level of extraordinary possibilities. It is a power that has allowed the ordinary to become extraordinary. It's a power that has placed a pauper on the throne. And that power is already present inside of you; just waiting for your command. Are you prepared and eager to *take charge* and make lasting changes? If you're not ready to take charge, like most young people today, don't worry; you also have the power to continue living on your self-created Island of delusions - do nothing. I recommend you put this little book down and continue to leave in denial. However, when tomorrow arrives, you realize that you have squandered a golden opportunity to rewrite your destiny.

The older men and women you see around you today were once your age. Majority of them ignored instructions that could have changed their fate. Most of them once lived on that disillusioned Island of self-destruction; they ignored the guideposts of wisdom as they journeyed along the path of life - pearls of higher wisdom that could have changed their destinies. Though, some tried but eventually gave up because the pearls of higher wisdom made no sense to them. And today, they are weeping hot, blinding tears of anguish and sorrow. They bemoan a yesterday that was lost because of paying heed to the wisdom of foolishness.

If there are aspects of your life that you dislike, either take responsibility and make necessary changes or continue to place the blame for those aspects of your life on everyone and everything else. Blame your parents, your environment, your skin colour, the economy, your low socioeconomic status, and your lack of education — in fact, blame anyone or anything. However, take no time to investigate the source of the problem - you.

You have the ability to overcome the difficulties you are currently facing. Stop pointing fingers at other people and start making the changes necessary to live the life you desire and achieve the outcomes you seek.

Taking full responsibility implies you acknowledge that all of your experiences—both successes and failures—are entirely your fault. It is easier to create the future you want to see when you accept full responsibility for your life and where you are right now. Instead of whining and putting the blame on others for your problems, you will be able to take control of your life. Give up using other people or external factors as excuses or justifications. Give them all up, for good.

You can make a difference, get things done correctly, and achieve the desired outcome. All that matters is that you make the right decision for yourself - you choose to be responsible for your life. And you will never give up on yourself, no matter what. Challenges cannot hold you back as long as you do not let excuses get in the way.

Take charge now and make a difference. Don't stifle your progress in life by harbouring destructive thoughts and engaging in self-defeating behaviours. Many young people today are quick to justify their failures with elaborate philosophies and illogical reasoning. They ignore useful suggestions that could help them improve. They are quick to engage in trivial activities that waste their precious time instead of actively seeking opportunities to constantly better themselves. As a result, most of them will be stocked in life tomorrow.

TAKE CHARGE NOW! Change can begin from where you are right now; it is up to you to take actionable steps to initiate the change that you wish to see tomorrow.

CHAPTER THREE
CHALLENGES ARE TEACHERS

In the school of experience, and as we journey through our destiny, we will come across challenges. These problems come our way to bring out the best in us. And for a student in the school of experience to advance to a higher level, that student must see challenges not as hindrances but as a passing phase of life. They are teachers sent to guide you to greater wisdom, but you must learn with humility and patience.

It is possible that a seemingly indestructible force or an invisible heavy chain is holding you down. And it is as if the force or the invisible heavy chain has severed you from your destiny. But that seemingly indestructible force and the invisible, heavy chain holding you down are not permanent. They still exist because you failed to understand their role as your teachers, and as long as you continue to be ignorant, the binding of the heavy chain will keep you in place. But you will not remain a failure if you are ready and willing to learn from the lessons that life challenges come to teach. If you are willing to learn, you will move on to higher wisdom, and your failures will vanish away.

If the night of challenges has descended upon you and your world is shrouded in pitch-black, impenetrable darkness, and you stumble along with a weary and uncertain step. I want you to know that the darkness that hides your glorious morning is just a shadow. No matter how dark your night is, it will truly awaken in the morning light. Darkness is unreal; it is a negative shadow that will surely disappear - it has no permanent residence. The impenetrable darkness and night of challenges that cast over you is a negative shadow that will undeniably pass over your life. Be an obedient child and learn from the school of life so that you do not remain in the dark and continue to suffer recurring punishments; disappointments and sorrows.

Don't let failure define you. Be willing to learn in the school of experience with obedience. So, you will not suffer because you are unaware of your true nature and the wisdom your trials should teach you. Many young people are unwilling to be freed from the shackles that have bound them. They are also unwilling or unable to make the personal sacrifices required to secure a grain of wisdom or long-term freedom. They shut themselves away in their darkened world, denying that the negative shadows cast over their lives will ever vanish. But there is light everywhere; it will set free those who want to be liberated from their darkness.

Challenges are your teachers. Endure learning what they come to teach and you will be equipped to weave them with a master's hand into the fabric that will clothe your future. And be willing to look into yourself; anyone who is willing to examine himself will find the courage to face his challenges.

CHAPTER FOUR
CHALLENGES ARE ESSENTIAL TO SUCCESS

A creeping, cancerous failure has enslaved millions of young people and their confidence has been eroded. Life's storms have battered them, they are staggering under the wings of challenges; only in death do they seek freedom. However, creative gold can be found in the leaden structures of difficulties. In reality, the leaden structures of difficulties are essential to success. The thing that seems like it would hold you back can actually set you free. Don't bemoan your limitations. Without clay, there will be no pots. Without oil, there will be no painting and without notes, there will be no music.

The challenges we face as mortals in this world are inevitable. Some are simple to overcome, while others initially appear to linger but eventually give way. There are difficulties everywhere; they are a necessary part of life and there is no life without them. But are these challenges genuine, untapped internal opportunities?

Challenges are hidden internal opportunities that, when properly understood and handled, will propel you to the next level of your life's journey. There is no champion who has not faced obstacles. It is not the trials you face in life that matter, but the conclusions you drew about yourself because of them; overcoming life trials brings out the champion in you.

Most time, people do not commit to finding solutions; instead, they only complain. Not that there aren't any answers or solutions to the issues that arose. But their inability to look for a solution and general laziness keep them down. Our problem is not a lack of resources, time, money, or opportunities; nature has kindly provided us with an abundance of resources and opportunities to ensure our survival. The restrictions we have placed on ourselves are the root of our problems.

No one is born inferior or useless; God blesses us. Nobody is truly poor; everyone is blessed in some way. We are created by HIM who exists outside the universe and still rules the world. HE is in nature, but is not nature, nor is HE bound by the laws of nature. Because we were created in God's likeness, no one is born without the necessities they need to thrive. We only become poor when we choose to do nothing about our problems. Being made in God's image and having access to the same creative power that he used to create the world gives each of us a unique makeup.

Anything you put your mind to, you can accomplish. Any height you want to attain is within your reach, but it must first begin in your mind. Have a clear idea of what you want to accomplish and the determination in the face of obstacles to stick with them. You are not poor because you are from a poor background. Rather, poverty has kept you from learning how to live above it. You are created for a purpose and you are expected to make a positive impact. However, you have the freedom to make your own decisions and lead the life you want.

The most important truth is that it's your life. Whatever you choose becomes your fate. But find the courage to make the necessary changes so that you can live the life you were meant to live. Challenges are essential in your life's journey; they are your stepping stones to success.

CHAPTER FIVE

BELIEVE IN YOURSELF

What happens to you doesn't really matter. It's about how you decide to respond to your experiences and the conclusions you make about yourself. Look past all the circumstances in your life that seem to be incorrect. They are not the end; you do not have to let them end your life. Doubting yourself and assuming that nothing you do is useful will ultimately lead to your demise. Even if you have unpleasant situations in your life, what good does it do to focus on them?

By focusing on the positive aspects of your life, you can find inspiration and courage to face the other negative sides you don't want in your life. Concentrating on what you have rather than what you don't have its advantages. You can decide right now to shift your attention away from those perceived "weaknesses" and start concentrating on developing your strengths; everything is under your control.

If you have faith in yourself, you can. You have the ability. You might not have what you want until you realize what you already have. Take a step to advance. A closed mind will prevent you from moving forward. So, let your best self shine through. With an open mind, you will recognize hidden internal opportunities, even when they come disguised as challenges.

As you focus on developing your strength, don't let those fleeting moments of unease deter you; instead, adjust the focal point of your mental camera. But when they do, refocus your mind's camera and look with the eyes of faith. The only person who can assist you is you. Only you can fight your battles. As a result, be brave and rise to the occasion, meet your challenges head-on, and believe in yourself.

CHAPTER SIX
TRY AGAIN

If you fail, try again! If you tried and failed, try again. Just try again and again. Those with trembling hearts will never succeed. Fear has reduced many promising young men to mere beggars. But you can, however, accomplish anything you want if you are fearless. All great achievers around us desired to obtain the object of their affection. They were confronted with trials, darkness, and struggles. Despite all this, they fought with courage and rose above their difficulties.

Try again; you won't believe in your abilities if you are afraid. You lose faith in your skills because you are afraid. And you are held down because you won't try again. Your internal skills are developing and regenerating. You can create the instrument you need to shape your destiny. However, if you let fear take root in your life, it will give rise to other types of fears. An abundance of useless weed seeds breeds more of the same useless weeds, like a neglected garden. fear, on the other hand, produces defeat and failure. Have the guts to bring about the victory you desire. Don't be afraid!

Your failure today does not mean you should never try again tomorrow. Tomorrow's success isn't limited by today's failure. However, the fear you carry today might limit your future success. Build your courage and faith; stop being afraid, but start using your courage and faith to discover your latent abilities. This will help you uncover your hidden powers and potential.

You have the potential to succeed in life because of your latent abilities. However, we are often too afraid to look inward to discover ourselves. Our fear of self-discovery binds us and turns us into willing slaves. Without purpose, we stray back and forth, not having any destination in mind. When you have no purpose in life, fear survives. You easily fall prey to worries and self-pity. But with a legitimate purpose in mind and with focus and courage upon the object you have set before you, fear disappears.

Reset the lens of your mind's camera; focus on your purpose and let its attainment become your supreme duty. Leave no room for ephemeral desires and imaginings. Even if you fail at your first attempt, don't give up, but try again. One day, your perseverance and efforts will undoubtedly pay off.

CHAPTER SEVEN
FOCUS ON THE VICTORY AHEAD

The vision you hold of yourself every day determines your success or failure. Your limitations are those you impose upon your abilities. By nature, you have everything you need to succeed in life. Look at the little sparrows; when they are hungry, they simply fly out there in search of food. They have complete faith and assurance that they will receive their daily meals. Never will you see them lose faith in supply. If they try here and are unsuccessful, they move on to somewhere else, but they will never stop searching. Daily, you see them flying from one place to another. Nature has never failed to provide for these little creatures. How much more you created in the image of God? Aren't you convinced you are much superior to these creatures? Look inside of you. What do you lack? What is holding you back from living your best?

Spread your wings with much faith and allow them to flap freely. God has given you authority and dominion. It is up to you to put what your creator has graciously and abundantly given you to good use. Hold the ideal situation you want to see in your mind with faith-filled eyes. Look at it and believe that it is yours. Spend your time every day, with faith, doing things that will bring you closer to the success you desire in life. If you believe you can succeed, no matter what obstacles you face, you will never fail. And obstacles will serve as stepping stones to propel you to your desired destination. But if you lose faith, you lose contact with God—you lose the perfect model of yourself that He has in mind.

Keep your focus on the victory; it is fruitless to lament your shortcomings or failures. Mourning over your failures or inabilities yields no results. Rise with boldness and change your situation with your faith-filled eyes. Begin today; now is the time to begin. There has never been a better time than now, and there will never be a better time than now. Yesterday is gone, and tomorrow is just a promise to come. Begin today, and you will arrive at a tomorrow that you will be proud of. Don't let your today hold you back from your tomorrow; fight back with all of your strength. Don't be distracted. Focus on the victory ahead.

CHAPTER EIGHT
IGNORANCE JUSTIFIES NO ONE

Ignorance does not justify anyone; it is not an excuse. Ignorance can shorten one's life. Many people stray in life because they lack knowledge; they lead a life filled with struggle and stagnation. The level of your knowledge determines your relevance. The level of your relevance determines your competence and ability to deal with daily life challenges. If you lack competence, what value will you be—first to yourself, then to the rest of the world?

If you are not competent, you will become irrelevant and useless - an object of ridicule only to be pitied. Your relevance depends on how you define and design your life. If you want to cross a lake and there is no means of getting across except by boat. The most sensible thing for you to do is to secure a boat. It will be most foolish of you to seek the other side of the lake when the proper thing for you is to seek the right boat that will take you across. If you get the right boat, getting across the other side of the lake becomes a lot easier.

If the opportunity you seek comes, and you don't have the required skill; how do you want to take advantage of it? Without adequate preparation, opportunities will only lead to failure, stagnation, and depression. But having the right skill and showing your ability will inspire people to come to your support. Realize that your relevance depends on your distinctive competence. So, go get one if you don't have a distinguishing skill.

Don't stop developing yourself and your skills, and don't be a slacker at work. People who succeed put in a lot of effort. Successful people put more emphasis on getting the job done than on having fun. Don't rely on others or put off what needs to be done right away; instead, put effort into realizing your dreams. Make working hard your guiding principle; successful people leave a legacy of perseverance.

Discover your natural talent, understand your areas of strength, and make the most of them. Play up your strengths and minimize your weaknesses. When you are in need of help, seek help so that you can strengthen your area of weakness. And make the most of every chance you get to advance and get better at what you do.

Put forth all of your effort to gain the knowledge and training necessary to help you achieve your aim. Associate with positive thinkers who will encourage you; learn from their experiences and wealth of knowledge. If you need to work under someone to gain practical experience, even if it means going without pay, please do so. The knowledge you will gain will be beneficial in the long run. Remember, ignorance justifies no one! Don't let lack of knowledge hold you down.

CHAPTER NINE
CONCLUSION

Nature provides abundance all around us. There is no such thing as a poor person; we fall short because we won't acknowledge our inner strength and seize it. There is an inner strength within you and the ability to achieve your aspirations - to become who you truly desire to be. However, activating that power and using it is your responsibility.

You don't have to be constrained, ineffective, miserable, or in need. Unpleasant circumstances need not decide your fate. The power to create the outcome you want is yours. You are made in the image of God and blessed with unlimited potential. You are not to be pitied. There is something great in you yearning for expression. It takes only you to discover it and bring it into manifestation.

Discovering and giving full expression to your ability will help you advance in your life's journey. However, as you make progress in your destiny, obstacles will arise to oppose you. But you must fight back without giving up. It is in the place of your assignment that you can advance, shine, and find fulfillment.

Great people view negative or disempowering circumstances as opportunities for growth and advancement. No experience should be seen negatively. The things we perceive as negative experiences help us grow and toughen our character. There are no mistakes, but only lessons. Have faith in yourself; use negative experiences as an opportunity to look inward and develop a better version of yourself.

Faith is the driving force, the assurance, the confidence, and the enforcing truth that can carry you to your destination. Your expectation can become a reality through the power of faith. Concentrate solely and fully on your dream and let faith, the power that lives inside of you, guide you to your destination. The world is waiting to see that great thing that only you can give to the world. Let the pearls of wisdom in this little book be your guidepost in your journey to freedom.

ABOUT THE AUTHOR

Kingsley Eleweke is enthusiastically involved in impacting young people through his teachings.

Contact him at:

Email: Primedgesolutions@gmail.com

Social: www.facebook.com/powisdomseries

www.ingramcontent.com/pod-product-compliance
Lightning Source LLC
Chambersburg PA
CBHW060510160726
47992CB00003B/1411